I0463262

111 Questions to Design Learning
Copyright© 2010 Kimberly Seeger

$16.95 USA
ISBN-13:
978-1456548513

ISBN-10:
1456548514

Author:	Kimberly Seeger, M.S. CPLP
Editor:	Melissa Terrell, M.S.
Graphics:	Mindi Zachary Talley
	www.MTdesignZ.com

The publisher offers discounts for quantity orders of the book. For more information contact:
Director of Business Development
Learniappe Publishing
1-225-266-0599

PRINTED IN THE UNITED STATES OF AMERICA
First Edition

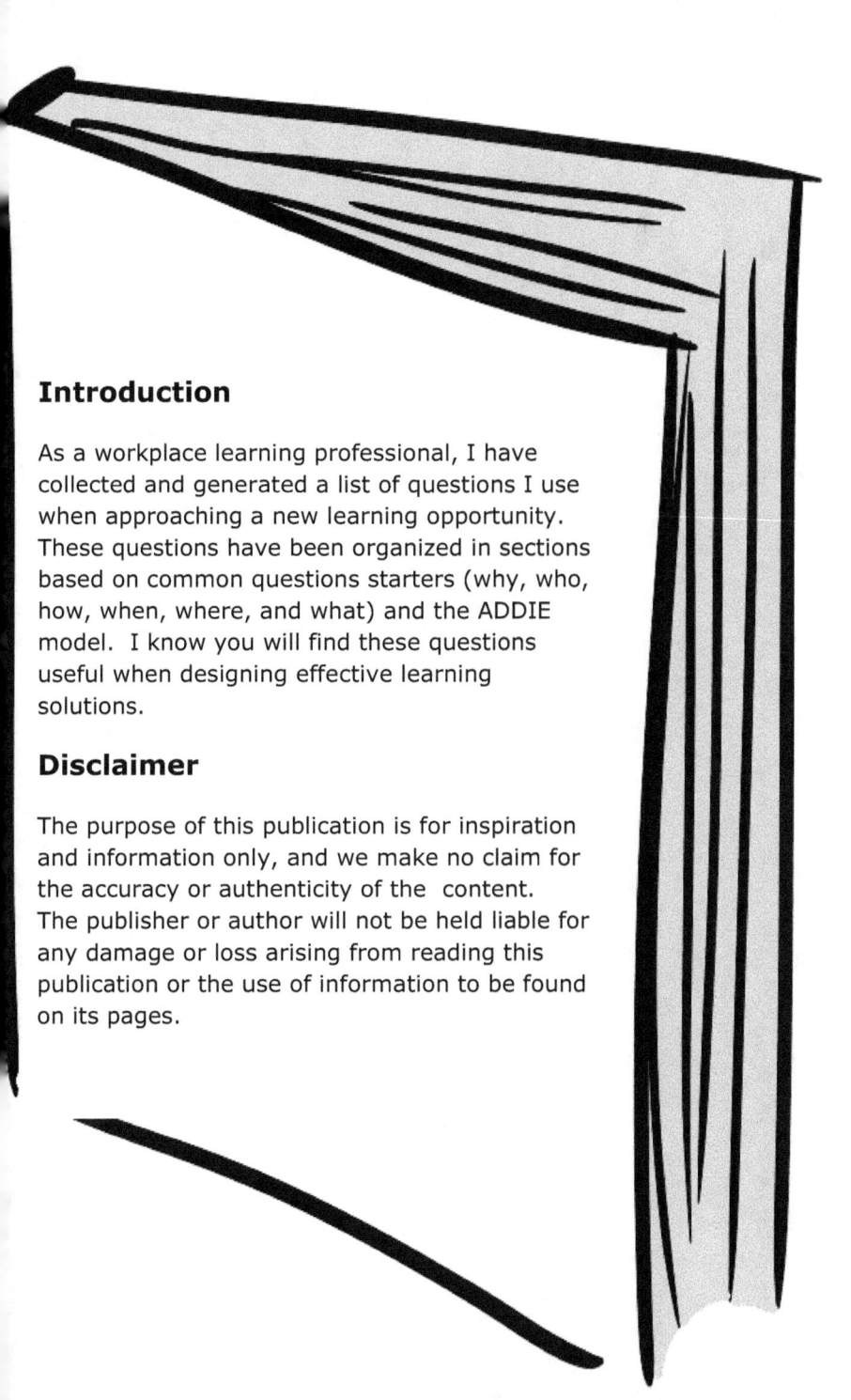

Introduction

As a workplace learning professional, I have collected and generated a list of questions I use when approaching a new learning opportunity. These questions have been organized in sections based on common questions starters (why, who, how, when, where, and what) and the ADDIE model. I know you will find these questions useful when designing effective learning solutions.

Disclaimer

111 Questions to Design Learning

Where do you begin when facing a new learning opportunity? By asking questions, of course! This book contains 111 Questions which provides a foundation for designing an effective learning solution.

Will you need to ask ALL 111 Questions? No! Only ask <u>relevant</u> questions to your learning opportunity.

- Why do you ask?
- Who do you ask?
- How do you ask?
- When do you ask?
- Where do you ask?
- What do you ask?

Contents

Designing learning requires you to listen to
more than the experts, data and words.
Listen for what is not communicated.

~ Kimberly Seeger

Why do you ask?

Good questions lead to effective solutions. Learning is an essential component of personal and professional development, therefore investing time and resources to understand what needs to be learned and how to deliver it will result in success.

- Why do you ask questions?
- Why do people prefer to be asked, not told?
- Why do people agree with their own ideas?
- Why are there misunderstandings?
- Why is there resistance?

One of the greatest tools to achieve success is asking questions. Why you might ask? It's because when you're asking questions, you're seeking others opinions & you're also slowing things down in order to validate judgments & perceptions, which are often the source of misunderstandings & failure. So ask more questions, & you'll improve your success-ability.

Sardek Love

Who do you ask?

PEOPLE! People are involved, invested and important to the success of every new learning solution.

- Who will be learning?
- Who will be providing resources?
- Who will be influencing the outcomes?
- Who knows the topic (subject matter experts)?
- Who will support the solution?
- Who are the key stakeholders?

In a nutshell, ask anyone who has an interest or involvement in the process.

An expert knows all the answers - if you ask the right questions.

~ Unknown

The most successful people in life are generally those who have the best information.

~ Benjamin Disraeli

How do you ask?

This book follows the most commonly utilized design model, ADDIE, to outline the process and organize the questions.   As you identify the questions for your learning opportunity, consider the purpose behind the question. Listen and record responses.

- How do you ask (sequentially or randomly)?
- How will the asker's nonverbal actions influence the responder?
- How would the responder prefer to be asked?
- How will the question clarify the challenge or opportunity?
- How will the question relate to the desired outcome?

Learning is an active process. We learn by doing. Only knowledge that is used sticks in your mind.

~Dale Carnegie

When do you ask?

As soon as you become involved in a learning conversation, start asking questions. In the Analysis phase of the ADDIE model, you want to learn as much about the outcomes (what success looks like) as the scope of opportunity. As you move through the questions, you will find that ADDIE is not sequential. You may learn something which causes you to return or reference another phase.

- When do you ask?
- When do you need answers?
- When will the responder have an appropriate amount of time to answer completely?

Trainers must begin with desired results and then determine what behavior is needed to accomplish them. Then trainers must determine the attitudes, knowledge, and skills that are necessary to bring about the desired behavior(s). The final challenge is to present the training program in a way that enables the participants not only to learn what they need to know but also to react favorably to the program.

~Dr. Donald Kirkpatrick

Where do you ask?

Asking questions in person, by phone or using virtual tools can all be very effective. Choose the environment based upon the relationship and desired outcome.

Ideally, face-to-face individual conversations will often generate factual information as well as candid, intuitive reactions. When working in a group setting, try to assemble people into pairs to generate ideas around specific questions.

- Where do you ask questions?
- Where do you record responses?
- Where will information be stored and shared?
- Where will the ideas be implemented?

Sometimes the questions are complicated and the answers are simple.

~ Dr. Suess.

What do you ask?

Questions!

Be sure to record responses for later reference. I recommend recording responses on index cards or sticky notes which can be sorted, prioritized, re-arranged and easily transported. Another suggestion is to video tape the conversation. You may learn much more from listening to the tapes than in the first conversation.

- What questions are relevant to this learning opportunity?
- What questions have already been asked?
- What questions have already been answered?

We learn more by looking for the answer to a question and not finding it than we do from learning the answer itself.

~ Lloyd Alexander

THE ADDIE MODEL

(Analyze, Design, Develop, Implement, Evaluate)

Analyze

Outcomes

1. What results are needed?
2. How would success be determined?
3. When do people need to know or do to achieve results? When is the deadline?
4. What should learners know (knowledge), do (skills) or feel (attitudes)?
5. How will learners be evaluated on their learning?
6. What outcomes will need to be achieved so that the return on investment (ROI) is positive?

Intent

7. Is training the best solution or a part of the solution?
8. What is the organization's objective, challenge or opportunity?

9. Tell me more about the challenge or opportunity?

10. What change is necessary?

11. How might we provide complete solutions?

12. What motivated you to investigate learning solutions? (trigger, stimulus)

13. What is the business need driving this learning initiative?

Influencers

14. Who will support the solution? (Leadership, informal influencers, etc.)

15. Who is the target audience (learners)?

16. What is the learners' background (experience, education, culture, expectations)?

17. How are learners dealing with the current challenge they face?

18. What are the learners' strengths?

19. How many people are involved?

20. Why will they be included?

21. Tell me about the learner demographics (age, roles, sex, education, culture, etc.)

22. How many have participated in similar situations/ training?

23. What are the learners' primary needs, challenges, pains or problems?
24. How would you describe the learners' attitudes, reactions and feelings towards the challenge or opportunity?
25. What delivery methods will meet the learner's preferences (instructor-led, online synchronous, online self-paced, etc.)?
26. What will the learners want to immediately implement from the training?
27. What do the learners already know (experience) about the topic?

Environment

28. What informal learning channels are established?
29. What are potential obstacles?
30. How will motivation and passion be sustained?

Resources

31. Who will design, develop, facilitate, evaluate?
32. Who are the subject matter experts (SME's)?
33. How long will it take to design, develop, implement and evaluate the learning solution?
34. What must be done, by whom and by when?
35. What resources are needed to sustain?

36. How much time away from regular work activities will be involved?
37. With no resource restrictions, what could be done?
38. What is the current budget?
39. What should your budget be to guarantee success?
40. Where might we find additional funding?
41. How might we save money or reduce costs?

You have brains in your head. You have feet in your shoes. You can steer yourself in any direction you choose. You're on your own. And you know what you know. You are the guy who'll decide where to go.

~Dr. Suess

Design

Learning Objectives (Outcomes)

42. Before this training, what should learners know or do? (pre-requisites, pre- work)

Environment

43. Where will the training be conducted? (virtual or live)

44. How might we make the environment engaging and interactive?

45. What tools/resources will we need?

46. When will learners need a break? (every 90 minutes physical break)

47. How would you describe the space? (virtual or live)

48. How might we make the space comfortable and safe? (virtual or live)

49. What functionality is available? (virtual tools, equipment)

Interact

50. What types of activities might help people remember and apply?
51. What communication methods might be used? (lecture, discussion, activities, groups, pair-share, simulations, teach-back)
52. What questions will the learners want to ask?
53. What questions might the learners ask the facilitator?
54. When should the pace be changed? (every 6-10 minutes)
55. How might we keep learners engaged and interested throughout the entire process?
56. What might be done to foster interaction and involvement?
57. What might be done to encourage networking and relationship building?
58. How might we create memorable photo opportunities?

Content

59. What standards of operation or performance should be referenced?
60. How might we make the content simpler?

61. How could we incorporate a theme?

62. What content MUST be included?

63. What content MAY be included?

64. How much TIME is allotted?

Facilitator

65. Who will be the trainer(s), speaker(s), facilitator(s)?

66. How would you describe their style?

67. What level of interaction do you want in the learning (1-10, with 1 lecture, 10 participants talking)?

68. How might we help the learners relate with other learners?

69. How might we help the facilitator learn more about the learners?

If the only tool you have is a hammer, you tend to see every problem as a nail.

~Abraham Maslow

Develop

Agenda

70. How will you manage the allotted time?

Interact

71. During this learning solution, what should learners know and do?

Process

72. How might we deliver the learning solution to make accessible and inclusive?
73. What might we do with the input and feedback produced from the learning solution?
74. How will your storyboard, design be documented?
75. Who will edit and approve?

Resources

76. What tools will the learners *need* to implement ideas and solutions?
77. What tools/resources have the learners *received*?

78. What tools/resources are *most useful* to the learners?
79. What job aids might we give learners?
80. What types of learner materials will be referenced? (workbooks, job aids)
81. What will the facilitator need to prior to the learning? (facilitator guide)
82. What visuals and graphics will be incorporated? (PowerPoint, flip charts, etc.)

It's a simple task to make things complex. It is a complex task to make things simple.

~Meyers Law

Implement

Process

83. What might we do to make it easy for learners to take action (do something with new knowledge, skills, and attitudes) and implement?
84. How might we follow up on the learners' needs?
85. How will we incorporate the learners' feedback?
86. How might we encourage the learners to take action after the training?
87. What have you done in the past to build excitement and encourage participation in training? What worked, did not work?
88. What types of advance preparation would learners be most receptive to completing (survey, reading, email, etc.)?
89. How will you "pilot" the training?
90. What must the learner do next?
91. What is the action plan?
92. How will learners be recognized?

93. How will success be celebrated?

94. How will progress be tracked?

Resources

95. What is the status of the budget?

I have been impressed with the urgency of doing. Knowing is not enough; we must apply. Being willing is not enough; we must do.

~ Leonardo Davinci

Evaluate

Results

96. After implementing this learning solution, what difference(s) will it/did it make for the organization?
97. What measures will indicate success? (examples include: increase sales, customer retention, employee turnover, reduction in processing time, decrease error rates, increase quality, reduction of accidents)
98. What is the ROI (return on investment)?
99. Were resources used effectively?

Behavior

100. Do the learners demonstrate behaviors in the workplace?
101. Do learned behaviors contribute to performance results?
102. Can the learners apply new skills and abilities to

effectively meet organizational needs?

103.What should the learner's leader and team members observe?

Learning

104.What knowledge will be/was acquired?

105.What skills will/can the learners perform?

106.What attitudes will be/were changed?

107.Are the learners confident?

Reaction

108. How do the learners feel about the learning solution?

109.Did the learners like the learning solution?

110.Was the facilitator engaging?

111.Was the learning environment (in person, virtual, etc.) appropriate?

The only man I know who behaves sensibly is my tailor; he takes my measurements anew each time he sees me. The rest go on with their old measurements and expect me to fit them.

~George Bernard Shaw

What questions would you like to add?

About the Author

Kimberly Seeger has designed, developed and implemented effective learning solutions for corporate, government and nonprofit organizations using practical tools and techniques. She facilitates workshops and presentations for organizations, conferences and professional associations. Popular requests include train the trainer, 9 Elements to Design Learning & Influence Behavior, Effective Leaders Flex.

Contact Kimberly Seeger for a presentation, workshop, coaching or design session, at 225-266-0599 or Kim@KimberlySeeger.com .

Kimberly invites you to connect:

Twitter http://twitter.com/KimberlySeeger

LinkedIn http://www.linkedin.com/in/kimberlyseeger

Facebook http://www.facebook.com/kimberly.seeger1

Blog www.kimberlyseeger.com

Website www.learniappe.com

To order additional copies of this publication or explore other designing learning tools, please visit:

www.learniappe.com

eNews: Learniappe distributes periodic electronic newsletters distributed by email subscription. The newsletter contains tools and techniques to design and facilitate learning. Subscribe at www.learniappe.com .

Learniappe Publishing
2010

Special Thanks

Thank you to all of the fabulous instructional designers, learning innovators and workplace professionals who asked me questions and contributed to this book.

Thank you to Gerald Haman and the KnowBrainer for inspiring innovative Questions.

References:

Dr. Donald Kirkpatrick's
4 Levels of Evaluation
http://www.kirkpatrickpartners.com/

Dr. Benjamin Bloom
Bloom's Taxonomy

KnowBrainer
www.solutionpeople.com